THE ULTIMATE SURVIVAL GUIDE FOR BEGINNERS

CHARLES G. BOOHER

Copyright © 2024 Charles G. Booher
All rights reserved
First Edition

PAGE PUBLISHING
Conneaut Lake, PA

First originally published by Page Publishing 2024

ISBN 979-8-89157-796-1 (pbk)
ISBN 979-8-89157-816-6 (digital)

Printed in the United States of America

CONTENTS

Introduction..v

Chapter 1: The Importance of Emergency Food and
            Water Storage..1

Chapter 2: Building a Comprehensive Emergency Food
            Storage Plan 4

Chapter 3: Efficiently Packing and Storing Your
            Emergency Food Supplies.................10

Chapter 4: Storing and Maintaining Your Emergency
            Supplies...15

Chapter 5: Bugging Out and Portable Emergency Supplies........20

Chapter 6: First Aid and Medical Preparedness 25

Chapter 7: Hygiene and Personal Care in Emergency
            Situations..29

Chapter 8: Cooking, Utensils, and Stoves in Emergency
            Situations..35

Chapter 9: Shelters..40

Chapter 10: Backpack Essentials and Preparedness....................43

Chapter 11: Hunting, Fishing, and Trapping for Survival 47

Chapter 12: Fires and Water: Essentials for Survival....................51

Chapter 13: Vehicle Preparations for Emergencies and
            Outdoor Adventures..............................56

Chapter 14: Essential Items for Emergencies and Natural
            Disasters...59

Chapter 15: Useful Websites, Shopping Tips, and
            Essential Items for Long-Term Storage and
            Preparedness...62

Chapter 16: The Journey to Self-Reliance: Overcoming
            Challenges and Embracing Technology 68

INTRODUCTION

In today's unpredictable world, it is crucial to be prepared for any emergency or disaster that may come your way. From natural disasters like hurricanes, earthquakes, and tornadoes, to man-made crises, such as power outages, economic collapse, and civil unrest, the potential for emergencies to strike is ever-present. Being properly prepared can mean the difference between life and death, making it imperative that you take the time to learn how to prepare yourself and your family for any situation.

The Ultimate Survival Guide for Beginners is a comprehensive resource that provides practical advice on how to prepare for any type of emergency. Whether you're a beginner or an experienced prepper, this book covers all the fundamental aspects of emergency preparedness.

One of the key topics covered in this book is creating a basic checklist of essential items. The author provides detailed information on the types of supplies that should be included in your emergency kit, such as food, water, first aid kits, and hygiene supplies. They also provide tips on how to store these supplies properly, to ensure they remain fresh and usable for an extended time.

In addition to these basic necessities, the book also covers more advanced preparation techniques, such as creating a bugout bag, designing a long-term survival plan, and even how to construct a makeshift shelter in the event of an emergency.

Another important topic covered in this book is how to maintain a calm and levelheaded attitude during emergencies. The author provides guidance on how to keep your family's morale up and how to prepare your children for such situations. They also stress the importance of staying informed and keeping up to date on news and information related to the emergency.

The book also addresses the question of whether to stay put or evacuate in the event of an emergency. The author provides detailed information on how to assess the situation, weigh the risks and benefits, and make an informed decision. They also discuss the importance of having a predetermined meeting place for your family in the event that you get separated during an emergency.

The author's extensive experience in emergency preparedness along with camping, hiking, fishing, and hunting also comes in handy when it comes to survival skills in the wilderness. They provide detailed information on how to build a fire, catch food, and construct shelter using natural materials.

Most importantly, the book emphasizes the importance of being financially prepared for emergencies. The author provides tips on how to save money and find great deals to make emergency preparation affordable for everyone, regardless of their budget. They also discuss the importance of having insurance and how to properly document your belongings to ensure you can receive proper compensation in the event of damage or loss.

In a world where only 10 percent of the population is prepared for emergencies, *The Ultimate Survival Guide for Beginners* is a must-read for anyone who wants to ensure their survival in case of a crisis. Whether you're a parent, college student, or retiree, this book is a valuable resource that can help you prepare for anything that may come your way. So sit back and enjoy this comprehensive guide that could potentially save your life and your family's.

CHAPTER 1

THE IMPORTANCE OF EMERGENCY FOOD AND WATER STORAGE

In today's increasingly uncertain world, it is essential to be prepared for unforeseen events and emergencies. Natural disasters, pandemics, and social unrest are just examples of situations that can disrupt our normal routines and access to essential resources like food and water. This chapter will provide an in-depth look at the importance of emergency food and water storage and offer tips on how to start building your own supply.

The necessity of being prepared

Being prepared for emergencies is not only a smart decision but also a responsible one. Ensuring that you and your family have access to food and water during times of crisis can be the difference between life and death. Moreover, having a well-stocked emergency supply helps alleviate the burden on already-strained resources during a disaster, allowing aid organizations to focus on helping those most in need.

Assessing your needs

Before starting your emergency food and water storage, it is crucial to assess your specific needs. Factors to consider include the size of your family, dietary restrictions, and personal preferences. Additionally, you should think about how long you want your emergency supply to last—generally, it is recommended to have at least a two-week supply of food and water on hand.

Storing food

When choosing food to store, prioritize items with a long shelf life, such as canned goods, dried foods, and nonperishable items. Diversify your supply with a mix of proteins, carbohydrates, and healthy fats to ensure a balanced diet during an emergency. Additionally, consider investing in vacuum-sealed or Mylar bags to protect your food from air, moisture, and pests. These bags can be used to create smaller individual portions, making it easier to access and consume your stored food without exposing the entire supply to potential contaminants.

Storing water

The average person needs approximately one gallon of water per day for drinking and hygiene purposes. Therefore, when planning your emergency water supply, aim for a minimum of fourteen gallons per person. Store water in food-grade containers, away from direct sunlight and heat sources. To keep water quality, replace your stored water every six months or use water purification tablets to extend its shelf life.

Storing and organizing supplies

Proper organization and storage of your emergency food and water supply are essential to ensure easy access and prevent spoilage. Keep your supplies in a cool dark place, such as a basement, closet, or under the bed. Organize items by expiration date, with the soonest-to-expire items at the front, to make sure they are consumed first. Label each container with its contents and expiration date for easy reference.

Emergency food and water storage is a critical aspect of preparedness that should not be overlooked. By assessing your needs, choosing long-lasting food items, and properly storing and organizing your supplies, you can ensure that you and your family are better equipped to face unexpected emergencies. This investment in your safety and well-being can offer peace of mind and serve as a vital resource during times of crisis.

CHAPTER 2

BUILDING A COMPREHENSIVE EMERGENCY FOOD STORAGE PLAN

Creating a comprehensive emergency food storage plan requires careful thought and consideration of numerous factors, such as nutritional needs, shelf life, and ease of preparation. In this chapter, we will explore the different types of food to include in your emergency storage, discuss proper packaging and storage techniques, and provide suggestions for customizing your plan based on the specific needs of your household.

Selecting the right foods

A well-rounded emergency food storage plan should include a variety of food items to supply adequate nutrition and maintain morale during a crisis. Consider the following types of food when building your emergency supply:

- Nonperishable items: Canned goods, such as fruits, vegetables, and meats, have a long shelf life and provide essential nutrients. Ensure your supply includes a diverse selection to prevent food fatigue.
- Dried foods: Beans, rice, pasta, and grains are staple items in many emergency food storage plans due to their long shelf life, nutritional value, and versatility. These items can

be combined with canned or fresh ingredients to create a variety of meals.

- Freeze-dried and dehydrated foods: While more expensive than other options, freeze-dried and dehydrated foods offer an excellent source of nutrition with a long shelf life. They are lightweight, compact, and easy to prepare, making them ideal for situations where space is limited or evacuation is necessary.
- Snacks and comfort foods: Incorporating familiar snacks and comfort foods into your emergency food storage can help maintain morale during stressful times. Items such as granola bars, crackers, and cookies can provide a much-needed sense of normalcy.

Packaging and storage techniques

Proper packaging is crucial for maintaining the quality and longevity of your emergency food storage. Consider the following techniques to protect your food from air, moisture, and pests:

- Mylar bags: These durable, metalized bags provide an effective barrier against air, moisture, and light. They can be heat-sealed to create an airtight environment, prolonging the shelf life of your stored food.
- Vacuum sealing: Vacuum-sealed bags remove the air from the packaging, reducing the risk of spoilage and extending the shelf life of your food. This method is particularly useful for preserving dried goods and other nonperishable items.
- Oxygen absorbers: Adding oxygen absorbers to your food packaging can help prevent the growth of mold and bacteria, further extending the shelf life of your stored food. Oxygen absorbers are available in various sizes to accommodate different types of packaging.

When storing your emergency food supply, consider the following tips:

- Keep food in a cool, dark place, such as a basement, closet, or under the bed, to protect it from heat and light, which can accelerate spoilage.
- Rotate your stock to ensure you are consuming items before they expire. Use the first in, first out method, placing items with the earliest expiration date at the front of your storage area.
- Label each container with its contents, expiration date, and any relevant preparation instructions.

Customizing your emergency food storage plan

A successful emergency food storage plan should cater to the specific needs and preferences of your household. Consider the following factors when customizing your plan:

- Family size: Adjust the quantity of food stored to accommodate the number of people in your household. Remember to account for any predicted changes, such as the addition of a new family member or the departure of a child for college.
- Dietary restrictions and preferences: Ensure your emergency food storage plan accommodates any dietary restrictions or preferences, such as vegetarianism, food allergies, or cultural preferences. This consideration not only ensures that everyone in your household will have something to eat during an emergency but also promotes a sense of comfort and familiarity.
- Meal planning: Plan out potential meals using the ingredients in your emergency food storage. This will help you identify any gaps in your supply and ensure that you have enough variety to keep meals interesting and enjoyable.

Expanding your emergency food storage

As you become more comfortable with your emergency food storage plan, consider expanding your supply to include additional items and resources.

- Gardening: Cultivating a home garden can supplement your emergency food storage with fresh fruits, vegetables, and herbs. Consider growing both seasonal and hardy, year-round crops to maintain a consistent supply of fresh produce.
- Livestock: If you have the space and resources, raising livestock, such as chickens, rabbits, or goats, can provide a source of protein and other essential nutrients. Be sure to consider local regulations and ordinances before committing to raising livestock.
- Canning and preserving: Learning how to can and preserve food allows you to extend the shelf life of fresh produce and meats, further diversifying your emergency food storage. Be sure to follow proper safety guidelines and procedures when canning and preserving food.

Keeping your emergency food storage plan up to date

Regularly reviewing and updating your emergency food storage plan are essential to maintaining its effectiveness. Consider the following tips for keeping your plan up to date:

- Periodically check the expiration dates of stored items and rotate your stock as needed. Replace any items that have expired. Meaning no longer eatable or consumed.
- Reassess your family's needs and preferences, adjusting your emergency food storage plan accordingly. This may include accommodating new dietary restrictions, family members, or changes in food preferences.

- Stay informed about new products, technologies, and best practices in emergency food storage. Continually educating yourself and incorporating new information into your plan can help ensure its ongoing success.

By taking the time to carefully plan and maintain your emergency food storage, you can better prepare your household for any unexpected emergencies or disasters. With a well-rounded supply of nutritious and familiar foods, you can help maintain your family's health and well-being during times of crisis.

To give you an idea of how to organize your dry goods within the five-gallon buckets, here are some examples:

Bucket #1:

- 2 x 5 lb bags of flour (in gallon Mylar bags)
- 2 x 5 lb bags of sugar (in gallon Mylar bags)
- 1 x 2 lb bag of salt (in half-gallon Mylar bags)
- 1 x 2 lb bag of brown sugar (in half-gallon Mylar bags)
- 1 x 2 lb bag of white rice (in half-gallon Mylar bags)
- 1 x 2 lb bag of dried red beans (in half-gallon Mylar bags)

Bucket #2:

- 10 lb of flour (in gallon Mylar bags)
- 4 lb of sugar (in gallon Mylar bags)
- 4 lb white rice (in half-gallon Mylar bags)
- 2 lb elbow macaroni (in half-gallon Mylar bags)
- 1 lb salt (in half-gallon Mylar bags)
- 2 lb red beans (in half-gallon Mylar bags)
- 2 lb pinto beans (in half-gallon Mylar bags)

Bucket #3:

- 5 lb of flour (in gallon Mylar bags)
- 2 lb elbow macaroni (in half-gallon Mylar bags)
- 10 lb white rice (in gallon Mylar bags)
- 2 lb pinto beans (in half-gallon Mylar bags)
- 2 lb of salt (in half-gallon Mylar bags)
- 4 lb of sugar (in gallon Mylar bags)
- 2 lb brown sugar (in half-gallon Mylar bags)

By dividing your dry goods this way, you can maximize your food storage and keep your supplies fresh for longer. This approach ensures that you have a variety of items available during tough times, without risking massive quantities going bad due to air exposure or contamination.

You can store various dried goods in Mylar bags, including potato flakes, pancake mix, pasta, oats, grains, and more. The choice of what to store depends on your family size and preferences. For spices, you can use small Mylar bags or 4 oz ball canning jars with a 100cc oxygen absorber. Organizing your spices in this way allows for easy and compact storage.

CHAPTER 3

EFFICIENTLY PACKING AND STORING YOUR EMERGENCY FOOD SUPPLIES

Properly packing and storing your emergency food supplies are crucial to ensuring their longevity and quality. In this chapter, we will explore various techniques and methods to help you maximize the efficiency and effectiveness of your emergency food storage. From using Mylar bags and oxygen absorbers to organizing your storage space, this chapter will provide you with valuable information to help you make your emergency food storage efforts possible.

Utilizing Mylar bags and oxygen absorbers

Mylar bags and oxygen absorbers are two essential tools for long-term emergency food storage. They work together to protect your food from oxygen, moisture, to light—all factors that can significantly reduce the shelf life of your stored food.

Mylar bags

Mylar bags are made from a durable and flexible material that supplies an excellent barrier against oxygen, moisture, and light. They come in various sizes, making them suitable for storing a wide range of dried food items, such as grains, pasta, beans, and powdered products.

When using Mylar bags, keep the following tips in mind:

- Choose the appropriate size. Select a Mylar bag that can comfortably accommodate the amount of food you wish to store. This will help prevent overfilling and ensure a proper seal.
- Clean the sealing area. Before sealing your Mylar bag, make sure the area to be sealed is clean and free of any food particles. This will help create a strong, airtight seal.
- Label and date. Clearly label the contents and date of each Mylar bag using a permanent marker. This will help you easily identify and rotate your stored food.

Oxygen absorbers

Oxygen absorbers are small packets that contain iron powder, which reacts with oxygen to remove it from the surrounding environment. Using oxygen absorbers in conjunction with Mylar bags can significantly extend the shelf life of your stored food.

When using oxygen absorbers, keep the following tips in mind:

- Choose the right size. Oxygen absorbers come in various sizes, measured in cubic centimeters (cc). The size you need will depend on the volume of the Mylar bag and the type of food you are storing.
- Work quickly. Oxygen absorbers begin to absorb oxygen as soon as they are exposed to air. To ensure their effectiveness, work quickly when packing your Mylar bags, and seal them as soon as possible.
- Store unused oxygen absorbers in an airtight container. To preserve the effectiveness of any unused oxygen absorbers, store them in an airtight container until you are ready to use them.

Organizing your emergency food storage space

Proper organization is essential to maximizing the efficiency and accessibility of your emergency food storage. Consider the following tips to help you organize your storage space:

- Use a first in, first out (FIFO) system. Arrange your stored food so that the items with the earliest expiration dates are in the front and easily accessible. This will help ensure that you are using your stored food before it expires.
- Group comparable items together. Organize your stored food by category (e.g., grains, beans, and canned goods) to make it easier to find specific items when needed.
- Label your storage containers. Clearly label each storage container with its contents and date to help you quickly identify and locate items.

Storing emergency food in various containers

In addition to Mylar bags, there are countless other types of containers you can use to store your emergency food. These include the following:

- Food-grade plastic buckets: These buckets are made from high-density polyethylene (HDPE) and are designed specifically for food storage. They are durable, airtight, and stackable, making them an excellent option for storing bulk food items. Be sure to use a gamma seal lid for added protection and ease of access.
- Canning jars: Glass canning jars with airtight lids are suitable for storing smaller quantities of dry goods, such as herbs, spices, and dehydrated fruits and vegetables. They provide excellent protection against moisture and light but be mindful of their fragility and potential breakage.
- Vacuum-sealed bags: Vacuum-sealing food removes air from the bag, which helps to extend its shelf life. This method

works well for items, such as dried fruits, vegetables, and meats. However, it may not be suitable for delicate items that could be crushed during the vacuum-sealing process.

Storing emergency water supplies

In addition to food, it is essential to have an adequate supply of stored water for emergencies. The following tips can help you store and manage your emergency water supply:

- Store water in food-grade containers. Use containers made from materials, such as HDPE or PET plastic, which are designed for food and water storage. Avoid using containers that have previously held chemicals or other nonfood items.
- Rotate your stored water. Although water does not technically expire, it can become contaminated or develop an unpleasant taste over time. To maintain the quality of your stored water, rotate your supply every six months to a year.
- Consider water purification methods. In addition to storing water, it is essential to have a method for purifying additional water in an emergency. Options include water purification tablets, portable water filters, and boiling.

Creative storage solutions for small spaces

For those living in small spaces, such as apartments or tiny homes, finding space to store emergency food and water can be challenging. Here are creative storage solutions to help you make the most of your available space.

- Utilize underbed storage. Use bed risers to elevate your bed and create additional storage space underneath. Store your emergency food and water in totes or other suitable containers and slide them under the bed.

- Maximize closet space. Use water bricks, food-grade buckets, or other stackable containers to create additional storage space in your closets. Place a piece of plywood on top of the containers to create a sturdy platform for storing additional items.
- Repurpose unused spaces. Consider using the space above your kitchen cabinets, under your stairs, or in other overlooked areas of your home for storing emergency supplies.

By following these tips and techniques, you can efficiently pack and store your emergency food and water supplies, ensuring that you and your family are well prepared for any unforeseen events. Proper organization, storage, and rotation of your supplies will help maintain their quality and maximize their shelf life, providing you with peace of mind in times of crisis.

CHAPTER 4

STORING AND MAINTAINING YOUR EMERGENCY SUPPLIES

Proper storage and maintenance of your emergency supplies are crucial to ensure their usability and longevity. To create a storage plan, consider the following factors:

- Space: Assess the available space in your home and find areas where you can store your emergency supplies. These areas should be cool, dry, and away from direct sunlight or temperature fluctuations.
- Accessibility: Ensure that your supplies are easily accessible in case of an emergency. Avoid storing them in hard-to-reach places or behind heavy or cluttered objects.
- Organization: Organize your supplies so you can easily find and retrieve items when needed. Label containers and shelves with the contents and expiration dates to help you keep track of your inventory.
- Rotation: Regularly rotate your supplies to prevent spoilage or waste. Consume items nearing their expiration dates and replace them with fresh supplies.

Storing food and water

Food and water are essential components of your emergency supplies. Proper storage practices can help prevent spoilage and ensure their availability when needed.

- Food: Store nonperishable, low-maintenance foods, such as canned goods, dried fruits, and freeze-dried meals. Avoid storing foods that require refrigeration or have a short shelf life. Keep food in airtight containers, and protect them from pests, moisture, and temperature fluctuations.
- Water: Store at least one gallon of water per person per day for a minimum of three days. Use food-grade water storage containers and avoid using containers that previously held chemicals or toxic substances. Store water away from direct sunlight or heat sources to prevent bacterial growth or chemical leaching.

Storing medical and hygiene supplies

Maintaining personal hygiene and having access to medical supplies during an emergency can help prevent illness or injury. Store medical and hygiene supplies in a clean, dry location, and ensure they are easily accessible in case of an emergency.

- Medical supplies: Stock a first aid kit with essential items, such as adhesive bandages, gauze, tweezers, scissors, antiseptic wipes, and pain relievers. Include any prescription medications or over-the-counter medications your family members may need.
- Hygiene supplies: Store personal hygiene items, such as soap, toothpaste, toothbrushes, toilet paper, and feminine hygiene products. Include hand sanitizer and disposable gloves to help prevent the spread of germs during an emergency.

Storing tools and equipment

Tools and equipment can be invaluable during an emergency, allowing you to perform tasks, such as cooking, repairs, or communication. Store these items in a secure, accessible location, and ensure they are well-maintained and ready for use.

Cooking and heating equipment: Store portable stoves, fuel, matches, and cooking utensils in a cool, dry location. Regularly check and keep equipment to ensure proper functioning.

Communication devices: Keep a battery-powered or hand-crank radio, as well as fully-charged cell phones and backup batteries, in your emergency supplies. Store these devices in a waterproof container to protect them from moisture or damage.

Tools: Stock essential tools, such as a multi-tool, duct tape, rope, shovel, and hammer. Ensure that tools are clean and in good working order.

Regular maintenance and inspection

Perform regular inspections and maintenance on your emergency supplies to ensure their usability during an emergency.

- Check expiration dates. Regularly inspect food, water, and medical supplies for spoilage or expiration. Rotate and replace items as needed to maintain a fresh supply.
- Test equipment. Periodically test equipment, such as radios, flashlights, and stoves to ensure they are in proper working order. Replace batteries, fuel, or other consumables as needed.
- Reassess needs. Regularly reassess your family's needs and update your emergency supplies accordingly. Consider any changes in family size, medical conditions, or dietary requirements.
- Update documents. Ensure that important documents, such as identification, insurance policies, and emergency

contacts, are up to date and stored in a secure, waterproof container.

- Maintain tools. Inspect and maintain tools to ensure they are in good working order. Clean and lubricate moving parts and sharpen cutting edges as needed.

Storing supplies for special needs and pets

Do not forget to consider the unique needs of your family members and pets when storing emergency supplies.

- Special needs: Store any necessary items for family members with special needs, such as hearing aids, mobility aids, or added medications. Ensure these items are easily accessible and well maintained.
- Pets: Store food, water, and any necessary medications for your pets. Include items such as leashes, carriers, and toys to help keep your pets calm and secure during an emergency.

Educating your family

- Ensure that all family members are familiar with your emergency supplies and understand their purpose and usage.
- Discuss your emergency plan. Regularly discuss your emergency plan with your family, including where supplies are stored and how to access them in case of an emergency.
- Train in first aid and tool usage. Provide training in basic first aid and tool usage to ensure all family members can safely and effectively use your emergency supplies.
- Conduct drills. Practice emergency scenarios with your family to build confidence and familiarity with your emergency supplies and procedures.

In conclusion, proper storage and maintenance of your emergency supplies are essential to ensure their effectiveness during an emergency. By creating a storage plan, organizing your supplies, and regularly inspecting and maintaining them, you can be better prepared for any emergency. Don't forget to consider the unique needs of your family members and pets and ensure that all family members are educated and familiar with your emergency supplies and procedures.

CHAPTER 5

BUGGING OUT AND PORTABLE EMERGENCY SUPPLIES

In emergency situations, it may become necessary to leave your home quickly, also known as *bugging out*. In these cases, having portable emergency supplies and a well-thought-out plan is crucial for your family's safety and well-being. This chapter will discuss the importance of preparing for bugging out, creating a bugout bag for each family member, and planning an evacuation route.

The importance of bugging out preparation

While it is essential to have emergency supplies stored in your home, there may be situations where staying at home is not a safe choice. Natural disasters, civil unrest, or other emergencies could force you and your family to evacuate your home quickly. Being prepared for such scenarios is crucial to ensure your family's safety and well-being.

Creating a bugout bag

A bugout bag is a portable emergency kit designed to sustain you and your family for at least seventy-two hours. Each family member should have their own bugout bag, customized to their needs and abilities. Below are essential items to include in each bugout bag:

- Water: At least one gallon per person, per day, for drinking and sanitation.
- Food: Nonperishable, easy-to-prepare items that don't require cooking or refrigeration. Consider including energy bars, canned foods, and freeze-dried meals.
- First aid kit: A comprehensive kit that includes bandages, gauze, adhesive tape, scissors, tweezers, pain relievers, antiseptic wipes, and any necessary prescription medications.
- Clothing: A change of clothes for each person, including warm layers and rain gear.
- Shelter: A lightweight tent or emergency blankets to protect from the elements.
- Tools: A multitool, knife, duct tape, and rope or paracord for various emergency tasks.
- Lighting: A headlamp or flashlight with extra batteries.
- Communication devices: A battery-powered or hand-crank radio, as well as a fully charged cell phone and portable charger.
- Personal hygiene items: Toilet paper, soap, hand sanitizer, toothbrush, and toothpaste.
- Important documents: Copies of identification, insurance policies, and emergency contacts in a waterproof container.
- Cash: A small amount of cash in small denominations for emergency purchases.

Planning an evacuation route

Having a well-planned evacuation route is just as important as having a bugout bag. Consider the following steps when planning your route:

1. Find potential evacuation destinations. Choose at least two safe locations in different directions from your home, such as a family member's house or a designated emergency shelter.
2. Plan multiple routes. Plan at least two different routes to each destination to account for road closures or other obstacles.
3. Mark important locations. Mark the locations of essential services, such as hospitals, gas stations, and grocery stores along your routes.
4. Share your plan. Ensure all family members are familiar with the evacuation routes and know what to do in case of separation.
5. Practice evacuating. Conduct periodic drills with your family to familiarize everyone with the evacuation routes and procedures.

Bugout bag maintenance

Just like your emergency supplies at home, it's essential to regularly inspect and update the contents of your bugout bags. Check for expired food, medications, and batteries, and replace them as needed. Keep your bugout bags in an easily accessible location, such as a closet near your home's exit.

Preparing for special needs and pets

Do not forget to consider the unique needs of family members with special needs and pets when preparing for bugging out.

- Special needs: Include any necessary items for family members with special needs, such as extra medication, medical equipment, or assistive devices. Also consider creating an emergency contact list with information about their medical conditions, allergies, and required medications.
- Pets: Prepare a bugout bag for your pets that includes a food, water, medication, leash, and collapsible bowl. Ensure that your pets have proper identification tags and that their vaccinations are up to date. Research pet-friendly evacuation shelters or pet boarding facilities in your area and include their contact information in your evacuation plan.

Vehicle preparedness

In addition to bugout bags and evacuation routes, ensuring that your vehicle is well-maintained and equipped for emergencies is crucial. Follow these tips to prepare your vehicle for bugging out:

- Regular maintenance: Keep your vehicle in good working order with regular tune-ups, oil changes, and tire rotations. Ensure that your tires are properly inflated and that your spare tire is in good condition.
- Fuel: Always keep your gas tank at least half full, as gas stations may be unavailable or out of service during an emergency.
- Emergency car kit: Store an emergency car kit in your vehicle, which should include a first aid kit, flashlight, jumper cables, tire repair kit, road flares or reflective triangles, and basic tools.
- Maps: Keep updated physical maps of your area and evacuation routes in your vehicle, as GPS devices may not work in emergency situations.

Staying informed

Stay informed about potential emergencies and evacuation orders by signing up for local emergency alerts and monitoring local news and weather updates. Familiarize yourself with the warning signals and emergency procedures for your area.

Bugging out vs sheltering in place

Bugging out should be considered a last resort when sheltering in place is no longer a safe choice. Evaluate the risks and benefits of each option during an emergency and make the best decision for your family's safety.

Preparing for bugging out is an essential aspect of emergency preparedness. By creating personalized bugout bags, planning evacuation routes, and considering the unique needs of family members and pets, you can ensure that you and your family are ready to face any emergency situation that requires leaving your home. Regularly review and update your bugout plan to keep it relevant and effective.

CHAPTER 6

FIRST AID AND MEDICAL PREPAREDNESS

In emergency situations, having a well-equipped first aid kit and knowledge of basic first aid techniques can be invaluable. A comprehensive first aid kit should go beyond simple Band-Aids; it needs to be well equipped to manage a variety of medical situations. In this chapter, we'll discuss the importance of first aid preparedness, how to assemble an effective first aid kit, the basics of first aid training, and real-life examples that demonstrate the impact of proper first aid.

The importance of first aid preparedness

First aid is essential not only for daily use but also in emergencies, especially when minor injuries occur within your family. A well-stocked first aid kit can help avoid unnecessary trips to the doctor or hospital. In more severe cases, first aid can be lifesaving while waiting for professional help to arrive. Remember, it's crucial to call 911 in case of an emergency.

Real-life example: In the aftermath of the 2010 Haiti earthquake, many injured people relied on first aid administered by fellow survivors due to overwhelmed medical facilities. Immediate first aid can save lives and prevent further injury, especially when access to medical care is limited.

In the event of a natural disaster or other crisis, access to medical care may be limited. A comprehensive first aid kit can make a significant difference during these times. Moreover, having first aid skills and equipment can contribute to the well-being of your community, as you'll be able to assist others in need.

Assembling a first aid kit

A good starting point for a first aid kit is the Be Smart Get Prepared First Aid Kit Hard Red Case, 326 Pieces, which exceeds OSHA and ANSI requirements. This kit is available for around $35 on Amazon and can also be found at Walmart in the first aid or camping sections.

Another highly recommended option is the New 2024 Design-Survival Home/Workplace First Aid Kit. This comprehensive kit includes a tourniquet and other essential items. While it may be more expensive, the investment is worth it, especially when considering the potential benefits during an emergency.

To enhance your kit further, consider adding offline first aid apps or compact first aid books. These resources can supply valuable information and guidance when power is unavailable and your phone is out of battery. Some first aid kits come with these resources included.

When assembling your first aid kit, consider including the following items:

- Adhesive bandages in assorted sizes
- Sterile gauze pads and rolls
- Medical tape
- Tweezers and scissors
- Antiseptic wipes and ointment
- Pain relievers, such as ibuprofen or acetaminophen
- A digital thermometer
- An instant cold pack
- A space blanket
- A first aid manual or reference guide

Remember to check expiration dates on medications and replace items as needed.

First aid training and resources

Having a first aid kit is important, but knowing how to use it is even more critical. Consider taking a first aid course, which can provide you with essential knowledge and firsthand training for various medical situations. The American Red Cross and other organizations offer in-person and online first aid courses.

In addition to formal training, there are numerous offline first aid apps and compact books that can serve as valuable references. These resources can help and guide you through procedures when professional help is unavailable. Some first aid kits come with these resources included.

Real-life application of first aid skills

Having a well-stocked first aid kit and proper training can make a significant difference in daily life and during emergencies. Whether you are camping, hiking, or fishing, a comprehensive first aid kit can provide you with the means to treat injuries and aid others in need.

Real-life example, in 2013, a hiker named Gregg Hein found himself stranded and injured while hiking in the Sierra Nevada. With a broken leg, he used his first aid kit and survival knowledge to splint his leg and survive six days before being rescued. This example highlights the importance of having a first aid kit and the necessary skills to use it effectively in a wilderness survival situation.

Another real-life example, in 2017, during the Las Vegas mass shooting, concertgoers with first aid training were able to provide immediate assistance to the injured while waiting for emergency responders to arrive. This event demonstrates how having first aid knowledge and resources can be invaluable during an unexpected crisis.

In disaster scenarios, having first aid skills and supplies can make you a valuable asset to your community. For example, in the aftermath of Hurricane Harvey in 2017, trained volunteers played a crucial role in providing first aid to those affected by the storm.

First aid preparedness is an essential aspect of emergency planning. By assembling a comprehensive first aid kit and acquiring the necessary knowledge and training, you'll be better equipped to handle medical emergencies and contribute to the well-being of your family and community. Remember, being prepared for the unexpected can make a significant difference in life-and-death situations.

To extend your preparedness even further, consider these additional steps:

- Encourage family members and friends to take first aid courses and become familiar with your first aid kit.
- Regularly review and practice first aid techniques to ensure you're prepared in case of an emergency.
- Keep a first aid kit in your car, as well as at home, to be ready for any situation.
- Learn about emergency procedures and protocols in your community, including evacuation routes and emergency shelters.
- Stay informed about potential hazards in your area and develop a plan for different scenarios, such as earthquakes, floods, or wildfires.

By taking these steps, you'll not only be investing in your safety but also in the safety of your loved ones and your community.

CHAPTER 7

HYGIENE AND PERSONAL CARE IN EMERGENCY SITUATIONS

Maintaining good hygiene is essential not only for daily life but also in emergency situations. It contributes to overall health and well-being and can prevent the spread of illness and infection. In this chapter, we'll discuss the importance of hygiene preparedness, the supplies you should have on hand, and how to manage hygiene during a crisis. We'll also provide real-life examples of how proper hygiene can make a significant difference during emergencies.

The importance of hygiene preparedness

While basic hygiene practices like washing your face and brushing your teeth may be second nature, preparing for a crisis requires additional thought and planning. Ensuring you have enough supplies to maintain proper hygiene is crucial for staying healthy and comfortable during emergencies, such as natural disasters or extended power outages.

Real-life example: During Hurricane Katrina in 2005, the lack of proper sanitation facilities and hygiene supplies exacerbated the already-difficult living conditions for survivors. Inadequate hygiene can lead to the spread of diseases and infections, which can further strain emergency response efforts.

Essential hygiene supplies

To ensure you are prepared for a variety of situations, consider stockpiling the following hygiene supplies:

- Toilet paper: Keep extra toilet paper in your home, preferably in bulk. Opt for high-quality, multiply toilet paper for better comfort and cleanliness.
- Wipes: Stock up on baby wipes or moist towelettes for personal hygiene during water shortages or when showers are unavailable.
- Baby supplies: If you have infants or young children, keep extra diapers, baby ointment, and baby powder on hand.
- Bar soap: Although liquid soap is convenient for daily use, bar soap is more portable and takes up less space. Store bar soap in a plastic container for easy transportation and use in your first aid kit or backpack.
- Toothbrushes and toothpaste: Keep extra toothbrushes and toothpaste on hand for maintaining dental hygiene.
- Lotions, deodorant, and creams: Stock up on moisturizing lotions, deodorant, and creams for rashes or poison ivy.
- Over-the-counter medications: Keep a supply of pain relievers, allergy pills, and antacids for various ailments.
- Shampoo and baby powder: Maintain hair hygiene with shampoo and baby powder.
- Feminine hygiene products: Women should have an extra supply of tampons, pads, and other necessary products for their monthly needs.
- Other personal care items: Consider including nail files, hand creams, and other daily necessities in your emergency supplies.

Managing hygiene during emergencies

During a crisis, access to clean water and sanitation facilities may be limited. In such situations, it's important to adapt your hygiene practices accordingly. For example, if the power is out but you still have access to water, a cold shower can supply a refreshing and necessary cleanse despite the discomfort.

Create a grab-and-go hygiene kit containing essential supplies, including toiletries and medications, in a dedicated backpack or bag. This will make it easy to maintain hygiene if you need to leave your home in a hurry.

Hygiene preparedness for women

Women's hygiene needs can be more complex than men's, and proper preparation is crucial for maintaining health during emergencies. Having a dedicated bag with extra feminine hygiene products, as well as other personal care items, can help ensure that you're ready for unexpected situations.

In addition to feminine hygiene products, consider including other daily necessities, such as nail files, hand creams, and any items needed for children. A well-stocked emergency bag can provide comfort and peace of mind during a crisis.

Real-life example: During the 2010 Haiti earthquake, many women and girls faced significant challenges in accessing feminine hygiene products, leading to an increased risk of infections and other health complications. Proper preparation and having a dedicated bag with essential supplies can help mitigate these issues in emergencies.

Hygiene and mental well-being

Maintaining proper hygiene during emergencies isn't just about physical health, it also has a significant impact on mental well-being. Cleanliness can provide a sense of normalcy and control during chaotic situations, contributing to reduced stress and anxiety.

Real-life example: In the aftermath of the 2011 Thoko earthquake and tsunami in Japan, survivors who had access to hygiene supplies and were able to maintain a level of cleanliness reported feeling more optimistic and better equipped to face the challenges ahead.

Good hygiene is an essential aspect of emergency preparedness. By planning ahead and stockpiling necessary supplies, you can ensure that you and your family are better equipped to maintain physical health and mental well-being during a crisis. Remember to consider the unique needs of each family member, including women and children, and to create a grab-and-go bag with essential supplies to make it easy to maintain hygiene in any situation.

To further enhance your hygiene preparedness, consider the following tips:

- Educate yourself and your family on the importance of proper hygiene during emergencies.
- Review and update your emergency hygiene supplies regularly to ensure they remain fresh and functional.
- Discuss hygiene preparedness with your community, including neighbors and local organizations, to ensure that everyone is prepared for potential emergencies.
- Research local resources and facilities that may be available during a crisis, such as emergency shelters or designated hygiene stations.

Hygiene preparedness for men

Many men tend to adopt an *I'll-be-okay* attitude when it comes to hygiene during emergencies. However, this mindset can be detrimental to their health and overall survival. Men, often considered the *muscle* of the family, have a responsibility to provide for their loved ones and maintain their health to make sound decisions. Thus, proper hygiene is crucial for men as well.

Men need to pay attention to their hygiene, especially when handling tasks, such as catching and cleaning meat or fish. Ensuring their hands are clean is essential to prevent the spread of disease. Foot care is also vital, as men will likely spend more time on their feet. Investing in good boots and wool socks can help maintain foot health.

Mental health: The role of men in family dynamics

In addition to hygiene, mental health plays a significant role in emergency situations. Children and other family members often look to men for guidance and support during crises. Consequently, maintaining good mental health is crucial for men to be effective leaders in these situations.

One way to promote mental health during emergencies is to encourage a team effort. Working together, listening to different perspectives, and making informed decisions, as a unit can help alleviate some of the pressure and stress men might feel. Remember, the ultimate goal is survival, and a strong team dynamic will increase the chances of everyone making it through the crisis.

Balancing Hygiene and Mental Health for Men

By taking care of both their hygiene and mental health, men can better serve their families and communities during emergencies. Here are tips for men to maintain hygiene and mental health in crisis situations:

- Prioritize personal hygiene, especially when handling food or performing other tasks that could potentially spread disease.
- Keep feet clean, dry, and well-protected with quality boots and socks.
- Foster open communication within the family or group, allowing everyone to contribute ideas and suggestions.
- Encourage teamwork and collaboration, as working together can help alleviate stress and improve decision-making.
- Practice self-care and prioritize mental health, recognizing the importance of staying mentally strong during challenging times.

Men play a vital role in family and group dynamics during emergencies. Proper hygiene and mental health are essential for men to remain effective leaders and providers in these situations. By prioritizing personal care and fostering a supportive and collaborative environment, men can help ensure the survival and well-being of their families and communities during crises.

By taking these steps, you can help protect the health and well-being of yourself, your family, and your community during emergencies. Proper hygiene preparedness not only contributes to physical health but also fosters resilience and a sense of control in challenging situations.

CHAPTER 8

COOKING, UTENSILS, AND STOVES IN EMERGENCY SITUATIONS

During emergencies, one of the primary concerns is preparing and cooking food, especially when there is no power or gas available. This chapter will discuss safe and efficient cooking methods in such scenarios, as well as the essential utensils and stoves needed for optimal food preparation. Real-life examples and detailed explanations will be provided to enhance understanding and ensure a comprehensive guide to cooking during emergencies.

Cooking options: Indoor and outdoor

Indoor cooking during emergencies requires safe and efficient methods. A common possibility is a Coleman stove, which runs on propane and can be used indoor if proper airflow is in place. The one-pound propane cylinders needed for this stove can be expensive, so consider using an adapter hose to connect the stove to a larger twenty-pound or thirty-pound propane tank.

Another option is a portable butane gas stove, which is compact and suitable for indoor use near a window. This stove requires butane gas cylinders, which should be kept on hand. If you have a fireplace with a clean chimney or a wood stove, these can also serve as cooking options as long as you have access to wood.

Real-life example: In the aftermath of Hurricane Sandy, many families relied on propane stoves and portable butane stoves to cook meals indoors, keeping their living spaces well-ventilated to prevent carbon monoxide poisoning.

Outdoor cooking options include gas grills, charcoal grills, and various camping stoves. A popular camping stove is the EcoZoom or rocket stove, which burns small sticks and kindling. Other versatile stoves include the VidaLibre camping stove and the Solo Stove. These stoves can be found at retailers like Amazon, Walmart, and local camping stores.

Real-life example: During the California wildfires, displaced families often used camping stoves and portable grills at evacuation centers to cook meals while awaiting assistance.

Essential cooking equipment: Pots, Pans, and utensils

In emergency situations or when cooking outdoors, cast iron and stainless-steel cookware are the most durable options. Cast-iron cookware from brands like Lodge, which is made in the USA and free of lead, is highly recommended. Cast-iron frying pans and Dutch ovens are versatile and can be used for various cooking and baking tasks.

Real-life example: During the 2020 COVID-19 lockdowns, many people rediscovered the joy of cooking with cast iron, as it retains heat well and can be used on various heat sources, including campfires and stovetops.

As for utensils, stainless steel is the most durable and heat resistant choice. Items, such as large spoons, turners, ladles, whisks, and tongs, should be included in your emergency cooking kit. Other essentials include can openers, knives, strainers, pot holders, and measuring tools.

Real-life example: In the aftermath of the 2010 earthquake in Haiti, relief organizations distributed cooking kits with stainless steel utensils to families in need, as they are long-lasting and easy to sanitize.

Putting it altogether—building your emergency cooking kit

Creating a comprehensive emergency cooking kit is crucial for preparedness. In addition to the cookware and utensils mentioned above, consider including the following items in a large, watertight tote:

- Nut-cracking kit
- Mixing bowls
- Paring knife
- Sponges for cleaning
- Paper plates and reusable plastic cups
- Aluminum foil
- Dish soap
- Meat thermometer
- Bottle opener
- Cheese grater
- Kitchen scissors
- Pizza cutter

Do not forget a large stainless steel pot for cleaning and other tasks, such as laundry, washing up, or collecting water.

Cooking during emergencies and crisis situations requires planning, preparation, and knowledge of various cooking methods and equipment. By assembling a comprehensive emergency cooking kit with durable cookware, utensils, and stoves, you can ensure that you and your family are well-equipped to prepare meals and keep a sense of normalcy during challenging times.

Maintaining and caring for your emergency cooking equipment

Proper care and maintenance of your emergency cooking equipment will ensure its longevity and reliability during times of need. Follow these guidelines for supporting your equipment:

- Clean and season your cast iron cookware regularly to prevent rust and keep its nonstick surface.
- Keep your propane and butane cylinders stored in a cool, dry place away from direct sunlight and heat sources.
- Regularly check your cooking equipment, especially stoves and gas connections, for wear and tear or damage, and address any issues promptly.
- Keep your knives sharp and safely stored to prevent injury and ensure efficient food preparation.
- Replace any damaged or worn-out utensils with durable stainless-steel alternatives.

Real-life example: Many campers and outdoor enthusiasts prioritize the care and maintenance of their cooking equipment to ensure it still is functional and dependable on extended trips or during emergencies.

Cooking techniques and tips for emergencies

In addition to having the right equipment, knowing various cooking techniques and tips can make meal preparation during emergencies more manageable and efficient. Here are suggestions:

- Plan your meals in advance to conserve fuel and minimize cooking time.
- Use one-pot recipes, such as soups, stews, and casseroles, to simplify cooking and cleanup.
- If using a woodstove or campfire, learn to cook with hot coals rather than open flames for better temperature control and fuel efficiency.
- Master cooking techniques, such as steaming, boiling, and frying, as these methods can be adapted to various heat sources.
- Familiarize yourself with alternative cooking methods, such as solar cooking or Dutch oven baking, which can be useful when conventional cooking options are unavailable.

Real-life example: Following the 2011 Thoko earthquake and tsunami in Japan, many survivors had to rely on their resourcefulness and adapt traditional cooking techniques to the limited resources and cooking equipment available in emergency shelters.

By preparing in advance, assembling a comprehensive emergency cooking kit, and honing your cooking skills, you can ensure that you and your family are well-equipped to face any emergency situation that may arise. This not only enhances your resilience but also contributes to your overall well-being during challenging times.

CHAPTER 9

SHELTERS

In this chapter, we will delve into the critical topic of shelter during a crisis. There is often a heated debate surrounding the best course of action, and the following is merely my opinion. Ultimately, you need to make your own decisions based on your unique situation.

Sheltering in your home

Your home is the most desirable shelter since it contains all your preparations. Ideally, you should stay put as long as possible, only leaving when absolutely necessary. You can take measures to protect your home from external threats, similar to how you would prepare for a hurricane. For instance, boarding up windows or deploying hurricane shutters. However, in extreme situations like a Category 4 or 5 hurricane, evacuation might be the best course of action.

Real-life example: In 2012, Hurricane Sandy caused widespread destruction along the eastern seaboard of the United States. Many residents chose to stay in their homes, relying on their preparations to see them through the storm. Others had no choice but to evacuate, seeking shelter with friends, family, or in public facilities.

Securing your home

If you decide to stay in your home, it's crucial to take steps to secure it. First, find out if your neighbors are staying or leaving, and exchange phone numbers to keep communication. Cover your windows with materials like wood, thick black plastic, or carpenter trash bags to prevent light from escaping, and create peepholes to observe the situation outside. Keep a low profile during the initial days of the crisis and rely on information from neighbors and radio broadcasts to determine when it is safe to venture outside.

Supplies and secrecy

Your home contains all your supplies, so avoid leaving unless absolutely necessary. Be discreet about your preparations, and avoid discussing them with neighbors, friends, or even certain family members. You must prioritize the safety of your family above all else. If others know about your stockpile of supplies, they might come seeking assistance during a crisis, potentially putting your family at risk.

Evacuation and finding alternative shelter

If circumstances force you to leave your home, you will need to find alternative shelter. Hotels and motels may be fully booked. Family members might be too faraway. In such cases, consider campgrounds or national forests. Ensure you have essentials like tarps, tents, and sleeping bags, and try to find your shelter near a moving stream or body of water.

Real-life example: During the 2017 California wildfires, many people were forced to evacuate their homes and seek shelter in campgrounds or other public facilities. Tents and sleeping bags were crucial items for these evacuees, allowing them to weather the crisis.

Survival skills and resources

When forced to shelter outdoors, it is essential to have a basic understanding of survival skills. Familiarize yourself with the construction of makeshift shelters, fire-starting techniques, and identifying edible plants. Consider investing in books like *Bushcraft 101* by Dave Canterbury or *The Complete Guide to Edible Wild Plants, Mushrooms, Fruits, and Nuts* by Katie Letcher Lyle.

In summary, securing a safe shelter during a crisis is paramount. Your home is the best option, but alternative arrangements should be considered if evacuation is necessary. Acquire essential supplies and survival knowledge to ensure the safety of you and your family, regardless of the circumstances.

CHAPTER 10

BACKPACK ESSENTIALS AND PREPAREDNESS

In this chapter, we will explore the importance of having two distinct types of backpacks for various scenarios: one for emergencies and the other for recreational activities. It is essential to have a well-planned and well-stocked backpack for each family member, as it can make all the difference in a crisis or an enjoyable outing. We will also discuss the importance of including children in the backpack preparation process, as it helps them feel secure and involved in different situations.

Emergency preparedness backpack

It is crucial to have an emergency backpack for each family member, packed and ready to go at a moment's notice. This backpack should have essentials, such as clothing, nonperishable food items, and individual-specific supplies. For example, the backpack belonging to a person with diabetes should have extra glucose-testing supplies, insulin, and snacks tailored to their dietary needs.

Additionally, each backpack should contain a copy of personal identification (e.g., birth certificate and driver's license), a list of medications, and contact information for doctors and pharmacies. Including emergency contact information for family members is also crucial in case of separation during a crisis.

A real-life example of this concept is the California wildfires, where families had mere minutes to evacuate their homes. Having an emergency backpack for each family member allowed them to leave quickly without wasting valuable time searching for essential items.

Recreational backpack

The second type of backpack is for recreational activities, such as hiking, camping, or everyday use. Unlike the emergency backpack, this one can be loaded and unloaded as needed, depending on the occasion.

For example, during a camping trip, the backpack might include a tent, cooking gear, and a first aid kit. In contrast, for a day hike, it could contain a light jacket, snacks, and a water bottle. The recreational backpack should be tailored to the specific activity and individual preferences.

Selecting the right backpack

When choosing a backpack, it is essential to consider factors, such as the size, weight, durability, and price. A backpack should not weigh more than 20 percent of a person's body weight, according to the United States military. For instance, if you weigh 150 pounds, your loaded backpack should be thirty pounds or less.

It is vital to consider the weight of items when buying supplies for the backpack, as every ounce counts when carrying it for extended periods. Ultralight gear is available but can be quite expensive. It is crucial to balance quality and affordability when selecting a backpack and its contents.

Packing essentials

The contents of a backpack will vary depending on the individual's skill set and the situation. However, fundamental items should be included:

1. Knife
2. Hatchet or axe
3. Machete (optional)
4. Folding saw
5. Fillet knife
6. Tarp
7. Cordage (e.g., paracord)
8. Sharpener for tools
9. Water container and purification system
10. Cooking gear (stainless steel)
11. Fire-starting tools (matches, lighter, and magnesium fire starter)
12. Sleep system (tent and hammock)
13. Clothing, rain gear, and warm socks
14. First aid kit
15. Freeze-dried food

Other items, such as carabiners, sewing kits, emergency blankets, and fishing gear, can also be included. Depending on personal preferences and the intended purpose of the backpack.

Involving children in backpack preparation

It is essential to involve children in the backpack preparation process, as it helps them feel secure and in control during uncertain situations. Having their own backpack with personal items like a favorite stuffed animal or book can supply comfort and stability.

Moreover, it is important to emphasize the concept of teamwork during times of crisis or recreational activities. Each family member should have their own responsibilities and tasks, ensuring that everyone contributes and works together.

Real-life example—family backpacking trip

A family of four decided to embark on a weeklong backpacking trip in the mountains. They began by researching and buying the proper gear for each family member, taking into consideration the size and weight of each backpack.

The parents involved their children in the packing process, allowing them to choose personal items to bring along, such as a favorite book or small toy. They also assigned each child age-appropriate responsibilities during the trip, such as gathering firewood or helping with meal preparation. This involvement created a sense of teamwork and shared responsibility within the family.

During the trip, the family faced various challenges, including inclement weather and navigational difficulties. However, their preparation and teamwork allowed them to overcome these obstacles and enjoy a memorable adventure together.

Having well-prepared backpacks for emergencies and recreational activities is crucial for individuals and families alike. By selecting the right backpack, packing essential items, and involving children in the process, you can ensure that your family is ready for any situation that may arise.

Remember that everyone's backpack and preferences will be different, and it is essential to do your research and consult with experienced individuals to make informed decisions. The goal is to be prepared, stay safe, and enjoy the great outdoors or face emergencies with confidence.

CHAPTER 11

HUNTING, FISHING, AND TRAPPING FOR SURVIVAL

Hunting, fishing, and trapping are essential skills to have in survival situations when one is left with no other options for obtaining food. While these activities may be controversial for some, they can make a significant difference when stranded in a remote location. This chapter will discuss these techniques in detail, providing real-life examples and practical advice for anyone looking to improve their survival skills.

Fishing for survival

Fishing is an accessible and healthy way to secure a protein-rich meal for yourself or your family. There are numerous approaches to fishing, ranging from using a traditional fishing pole to crafting a makeshift cane pole or investing in a compact pole designed for backpacking. Regardless of your chosen method, it's crucial to carry a scaled-down version of a tackle box, complete with extra line, hooks, and lures.

Fishing techniques and tips

Fishing requires knowledge of various techniques and understanding the best times and locations for success. Valuable tips include the following:

- Fish in the early morning and early evening when fish are more likely to be active.
- Avoid fishing with the sun at your back to prevent your shadow from scaring fish away.
- Look for deep holes in rivers or streams, as fish tend to gather in these areas.
- Search for downed trees or lily pads, as fish often seek cover in these locations.

Bait and tackle

Finding bait can be as simple as searching under rocks or logs for insects and worms. In situations where live bait is scarce, artificial lures can be highly effective. When leaving fishing gear unattended, secure it to a stationary object to prevent loss. A helpful trick is to use a Y-shaped stick to hold the fishing pole in place and weigh it down with a rock or log.

Real-life example: Survival fishing in the wilderness

In one real-life example, in 1984, a stranded hiker in Yellowstone National Park found himself lost in a remote area without sufficient food supplies. Using a makeshift fishing pole and line crafted from found materials, he managed to catch fish from a nearby stream, providing him with the necessary sustenance to survive until he was eventually rescued after three weeks lost in the woods.

Hunting for survival

While hunting may not appeal to everyone, having access to a firearm can be beneficial for survival situations. For small game like squirrels and rabbits, a .22 caliber rifle is lightweight and easy to manage. For larger game or birds, a 12-gauge shotgun is versatile and capable of shooting different types of ammunition.

Hunting safety and ethics

It's essential to practice safe and ethical hunting, including familiarizing yourself with local hunting regulations, understanding the proper handling of firearms, and ensuring you have the necessary permits. Always treat firearms with respect and follow the following four basic rules of gun safety:

1. Treat every gun as if it were loaded.
2. Never point a gun at anything you don't intend to shoot.
3. Keep your finger off the trigger until you're ready to fire.
4. Be aware of your target and what's beyond it.

Real-life example—hunting for survival

In one instance, a group of hunters in 1991 found themselves stranded in a remote forest in Maine after their vehicle broke down. With limited food supplies, the hunters relied on their skills to hunt game for sustenance. By carefully rationing their ammunition and focusing on small game, they managed to secure enough food until they were eventually rescued after fifteen days.

Trapping for survival

Trapping can be an effective method for securing food in survival situations. However, it requires knowledge and experience to be successful. Various traps can be employed, including humane cage traps that allow for catch-and-release of unwanted animals and snare wire traps for catching small prey. It is crucial to educate yourself on proper trapping techniques and ensure that you are using ethical and legal methods.

Types of traps

There are several types of traps suitable for survival situations, including:

1. Cage traps: These traps are designed to capture animals without harming them, allowing for the release of nontarget species. Cage traps can be used for small game like rabbits and squirrels.
2. Snare traps: Snare traps are made from wire or cord and can be set up to catch small prey. These traps work by tightening around the animal's neck or body when it passes through the loop. Snares must be checked regularly to avoid unnecessary suffering.
3. Deadfall traps: These traps use the weight of a heavy object, like a rock or log, to kill or incapacitate an animal. They require careful construction and placement to be effective.

Real-life example—trapping for survival

In one example, a wilderness enthusiast found himself lost and without food in a remote area Canadian Rockies. Drawing on his knowledge of trapping, he constructed various traps to catch small game. By rotating between cage traps, snares, and deadfall traps, he managed to maintain a steady supply of food until he was able to find his way back to civilization.

In survival situations, hunting, fishing, and trapping can be vital skills for securing food. By learning and practicing these techniques, you can increase your chances of survival in challenging circumstances. It is essential to approach these activities with a focus on safety, ethics, and legality, ensuring that you are well-prepared to face any situation that arises. Always remember to familiarize yourself with local regulations and practice responsible resource management.

CHAPTER 12

FIRES AND WATER: ESSENTIALS FOR SURVIVAL

Fire and water are fundamental elements for survival in the wilderness. Whether camping, hiking, or facing unexpected circumstances, these two components can determine life or death. This chapter will discuss the importance of fire and water, how to create and maintain a fire, and how to locate and purify water, while offering professional insights and real-life examples.

Fire

Fire provides warmth, a means of cooking, and a sense of security. Knowing how to build and maintain a fire is crucial in any survival situation.

Fire preparation

Before starting a fire, clear the area of leaves and debris, and if possible, create a ring of rocks to contain the fire. Gather various sizes of wood, including tinder to ignite the fire, small twigs for kindling, and larger logs for maintaining it. If available, use the bark from a white birch tree, dried brown grass, or wood shavings as tinder. Always have a lighter, matches, or a magnesium fire starter available.

Building and maintaining a fire

To build a fire, place tinder in the center of the fire pit, and create two piles of twigs on either side in an upside-down V shape. Stack the next size of wood in front of the V. Ignite the tinder, and gently pull both piles of twigs over the flame, ensuring sufficient airflow. Gradually add larger logs as the fire grows.

Dos and Don'ts

Do
- collect enough wood to last through the night and first thing in the morning;
- keep wood dry and covered with a tarp or pine branches;
- maintain the fire consistently;
- have a tinder bundle on hand in a dry place, such as your pack or tent.

Don't
- attempt to start a fire with inappropriate materials, like newspaper and large logs;
- place the fire too close to your shelter (keep a two to three feet distance);
- gather wood in the rain or allow your wood supply to run out;
- let your fire go out, especially in wet conditions.

Real-life example: In 2012, a group of inexperienced campers found themselves in a cold, rainy situation without a fire. An experienced outdoorsman helped them collect suitable wood and started a fire using the techniques described above. The warmth and comfort provided by the fire greatly improved their experience.

Water

Clean water is essential for survival, and knowing how to find and purify it can be lifesaving.

Locating water sources

When looking for water, avoid stagnant sources like lakes or ponds, as they can harbor harmful bacteria and microorganisms. Instead, seek out springs or streams with moving water, which are less likely to have harmful contaminants. If the water appears murky or sandy, filter it through a cloth before purifying it.

Purifying water

Boiling water is the most effective way to purify it. Portable water purification devices and tablets are also available for convenience. Exercise caution when gathering water from large rivers, as pollution may be a concern.

Hydration in emergency situations

In extreme situations, if you have no means to purify water and are facing dehydration, take a chance and drink from the available source. The risk of dehydration is far greater than the potential harm from ingesting untreated water.

Real-life example: A hiker became lost in a remote area and was running low on water. They found a small, moving stream and used their portable water purification device to obtain clean drinking water, ensuring their survival until they were found.

In conclusion, fire and water are essential components for survival in the wilderness. By understanding how to properly build and maintain a fire, as well as locate and purify water sources, you can dramatically increase your chances of survival in any outdoor situation. Mastering these skills is invaluable, not only for recreational purposes but also for emergency scenarios when venturing into the great outdoors.

ADDITIONAL TIPS FOR FIRE AND WATER MANAGEMENT

Fire safety

Always practice fire safety to prevent wildfires and protect the environment. Ensure your fire is completely extinguished before leaving the site. Douse the fire with water, stir the ashes, and douse it again to make certain it is out.

Conserving water

In water-scarce situations, it's essential to conserve your water supply. Only use the necessary amount for drinking, cooking, and hygiene. Avoid wasting water by carefully rationing your supply and collecting rainwater when possible.

Staying informed

Stay up to date on the latest techniques and technology for fire starting and water purification. Learn from experienced outdoors enthusiasts, take wilderness survival courses, and read books on the subject to continuously improve your skills.

Real-life example: An experienced camper decided to participate in a wilderness survival course to further enhance their knowledge. During the course, they learned new techniques for fire starting and water purification, which proved invaluable during a subsequent camping trip when they faced unexpected challenges.

The importance of preparedness

Being prepared for any situation is crucial when venturing into the wilderness. Ensure you have the necessary tools, equipment, and knowledge to build and keep a fire, find and purify water, and respond to unexpected circumstances.

Essential items

Always carry essential items, such as a lighter or matches, magnesium fire starter, water purification tablets or devices, a tarp, and a reliable knife. These tools can be the difference between a successful wilderness experience and a potentially life-threatening situation.

Planning and practice

Before heading out on a wilderness adventure, plan your route, and familiarize yourself with the area, including potential water sources and hazards. Practice building fires and purifying water in a controlled environment so you're well-equipped to handle these tasks in the wild.

Developing a survival mindset

In addition to physical preparation, developing a survival mindset is crucial. Cultivate a sense of resourcefulness, adaptability, and determination. These mental traits, combined with practical skills, will significantly improve your chances of survival in the wilderness.

In summary, understanding the importance of fire and water and mastering the skills necessary to manage them effectively are crucial for anyone venturing into the wilderness. Preparedness, both mental and physical, is key to ensuring a safe and enjoyable outdoor experience.

CHAPTER 13

VEHICLE PREPARATIONS FOR EMERGENCIES AND OUTDOOR ADVENTURES

Preparing your vehicle for quick escapes or outdoor adventures is crucial. This involves keeping your vehicle's mechanical condition, ensuring its roadworthiness, and equipping it with essential emergency supplies. In this chapter, we will discuss the importance of vehicle maintenance, the essential items to have in an emergency vehicle kit, and real-life examples of how these preparations can be effective in challenging situations.

Vehicle maintenance

Proper vehicle maintenance is the foundation for a safe and reliable outdoor experience. Regularly servicing your vehicle can help prevent unexpected breakdowns and ensure optimal performance.

Basic maintenance

Stay up to date with routine maintenance, such as oil changes, tire rotations, and air filter replacements, to achieve the best fuel efficiency and prolong your vehicle's life. Routinely check your tire tread depth and pressure to ensure optimal traction and fuel economy.

Monitoring and maintaining your battery will ensure dependable starting in various conditions.

Real-life example: A group of friends planning a weekend camping trip made sure to service their vehicle and check the tire pressure before heading out. This attention to detail ensured a smooth journey and prevented any unexpected breakdowns.

Seasonal preparations

Depending on your location and the time of year, seasonal vehicle preparations may be necessary. In colder climates, consider using winter tires, checking the antifreeze levels, and ensuring the heating system is functioning correctly. In hotter climates, ensure the air-conditioning and cooling systems are working efficiently.

Essential emergency vehicle kit

An emergency vehicle kit should contain items that can help in various situations, from minor breakdowns to more severe incidents.

A well-stocked emergency vehicle kit should include the following:

1. Gloves: to protect your hands from cold or hot surfaces
2. Flashlight and headlamp: to provide light during nighttime emergencies
3. Warm blanket: to keep you warm if stranded in freezing weather
4. Road flares or reflective triangles: to signal for help and make your vehicle visible to others
5. Shovel: to dig your vehicle out if stuck in mud, sand, or snow
6. Come-along and tow strap: to assist in recovering your vehicle if stuck
7. First aid kit: to treat minor injuries during an emergency
8. Basic tool kit: to perform minor repairs on your vehicle

Real-life example: A family traveling on a remote road encountered a flat tire. Thanks to their well-stocked emergency vehicle kit, they had the necessary tools and equipment to change the tire and continue their journey safely.

Additional items

Consider including these added items in your emergency vehicle kit:

1. Jumper cables: To jump-start your vehicle if the battery dies.
2. Spare tire: A full-size spare tire is preferable, as a temporary *doughnut* tire has limited range and speed capabilities.
3. Tire pressure gauge: To ensure your tires are properly inflated.
4. Tire repair kit: To fix minor punctures without replacing the tire.
5. Portable air compressor: To inflate a flat tire or adjust tire pressure.
6. Extra clothing and rain gear: To stay warm and dry during emergencies.
7. Nonperishable food and water: To sustain you if stranded for an extended period.

Proper vehicle maintenance and a well-stocked emergency vehicle kit are essential for anyone venturing into the outdoors or traveling long distances. These preparations can make a significant difference in challenging situations and ensure a safe and enjoyable experience. By staying informed, practicing maintenance routines, and regularly updating your emergency vehicle kit, you can confidently face any situation on the road.

CHAPTER 14

ESSENTIAL ITEMS FOR EMERGENCIES AND NATURAL DISASTERS

Being prepared for emergencies or natural disasters is crucial for the safety and well-being of your family. In this chapter, we will discuss essential items to have on hand in your home with practical advice and real-life examples to demonstrate their importance.

Essential items for emergencies

The following items are recommended to have on hand to help you navigate through a natural disaster or other emergency situations.

Lighting

1. Flashlights: Provide one flashlight for each family member and have backup flashlights available.
2. Headlamps: These hands-free lighting options are useful when you need to perform tasks in the dark.
3. Battery-powered tea lights: Safer than candles, these lights reduce the risk of fire and can be used for ambient lighting.

Real-life example: During a power outage, a family with adequate lighting supplies was able to navigate their home safely, prepare meals, and keep a sense of normalcy for their children.

Communication

1. Battery-powered or crank radio: A radio with a built-in crank can be a reliable source of information during an emergency. Choose one with NOAA weather emergency capabilities to stay informed about severe weather conditions.

Real-life example: In the aftermath of a hurricane, a family with a crank radio was able to receive updates on the situation and make informed decisions about their safety.

Things to have on hand:

1. Contractor bags (3 mil or thicker): Useful for various purposes, including collecting debris, covering broken windows, creating makeshift shelters, and protecting belongings.
2. A hammer, nails, and utility knife: Essential tools for making repairs or creating makeshift solutions during an emergency.
3. Bleach and white vinegar: Useful for cleaning, sanitizing, and purifying water if boiling is not possible.
4. Disposable tableware: Paper plates, plastic cups, and plastic utensils can minimize dishwashing during an emergency.

Power and energy

1. Battery inventory: Ensure you have enough batteries for all devices, and purchase extra to be on the safe side.

2. Portable battery-powered charger or solar charger: Keep your phone charged during an emergency, ensuring communication with the outside world.
3. Generator: A generator can help maintain power to essential appliances, such as refrigerators, during a power outage.

Real-life example: A family with a generator managed to keep their refrigerator running during an extended power outage, preserving their food supply and minimizing financial loss.

Miscellaneous items

1. Gas cans: Store at least two five-gallon gas cans for your generator.
2. Cooler: Keep perishable food and drinks cold without opening the refrigerator frequently.
3. Waterproof notepad: Write important information, such as emergency contacts, that can be accessed even in wet conditions.
4. Duct tape: A versatile tool for repairs and makeshift solutions during emergencies.

Having essential items on hand for emergencies and natural disasters can make a significant difference in your family's safety, well-being, and ability to cope during challenging situations. By ensuring you have adequate lighting, communication, cleaning supplies, power sources, and other miscellaneous items, you can face emergencies with confidence and be better prepared to protect your loved ones. Regularly review and update your emergency supplies to ensure that you are always ready for unexpected situations.

CHAPTER 15

USEFUL WEBSITES, SHOPPING TIPS, AND ESSENTIAL ITEMS FOR LONG-TERM STORAGE AND PREPAREDNESS

In this chapter, we will provide you with a comprehensive list of useful websites for purchasing emergency supplies, coupon websites to save money, and essential items for long-term storage to help you prepare for any emergency or natural disaster. We will also discuss specific items to include in your emergency backpack and provide real-life examples to illustrate their importance.

Recommended websites for emergency supplies and savings

The following websites offer a wide range of products and services for emergency preparedness and long-term storage. Additionally, we have included coupon websites to help you save money on your purchases.

Websites for Emergency Supplies

1.   www.amazon.com
2.   www.walmart.com
3.   www.cabelas.com
4.   www.basspro.com

5. www.ebay.com
6. www.lodge.com
7. www.homedepot.com
8. www.lowes.com
9. www.target.com
10. www.etsy.com

Coupon websites

1. www.smartsource.com
2. www.coolsavings.com
3. www.grocerysmarts.com
4. www.grocerycouponnetwork.com
5. www.ppgazette.com
6. www.redplum.com
7. www.mambosprouts.com
8. www.coupons.com
9. www.couponmom.com
10. www.valpak.com

Essential items for long-term storage

Preparing a stockpile of canned and dried goods for long-term storage is essential for emergency preparedness. The following lists will provide you with a comprehensive selection of canned and dried goods that can be stored for extended periods.

Canned goods for long-term storage

1. Chef Boyardee products
2. Canned vegetables (any variety)
3. Canned beans (any variety)
4. Vienna sausage
5. Canned chicken in water
6. Canned ham
7. Campbell's Chunky soups

8. Corned beef hash
9. Canned chili
10. Canned potatoes
11. SpaghettiOs
12. Canned tuna fish in water
13. Spam
14. Canned roast beef
15. Canned pulled pork
16. Canned salmon
17. Canned sardines
18. Canned fruit (watch end dates and acidity levels)
19. Canned tomatoes and sauce
20. Canned beef stew
21. Canned chicken and dumplings
22. Canned gravy

Dried goods for long-term storage

1. Flour, sugar, and salt
2. Spaghetti and pasta
3. Oats and cornmeal
4. Beans and white rice
5. Whole wheat
6. Dried berries (all varieties)
7. Cereals (all varieties)
8. Powdered milk
9. Whole spices
10. Rye and barley
11. Dehydrated vegetables
12. Dehydrated meats
13. Baking powder
14. Yeast
15. Baking soda
16. Cocoa powder
17. Pepper

Essential items for your emergency Backpack

An emergency backpack should have essential items to aid in your survival during an emergency or natural disaster. The following list provides a comprehensive selection of items to include in your emergency backpack.

1. Carabiner clips
2. Emergency blanket
3. Emergency flares
4. P-38 and P-51 can openers
5. Flint and steel
6. Campsite storage strap
7. LED flashlight (1800 lumens)
8. Extra tarp
9. Microfiber towel
10. Extra socks
11. Waterproof notepad
12. Waterproof pen
13. Pack grills
14. A good pair of gloves
15. A good compass
16. Waterproof hat with brim
17. Protective glasses
18. Snare traps
19. Fire blower pipe
20. Pack solar charger
21. Small pry bar
22. Dew rags
23. Utilities key
24. Construction ignition key set
25. Cotton balls
26. Small bottle of Vaseline
27. Trioxane fuel bars
28. Foraging pouch
29. Headlamp

30. Stainless steel pot
31. Fishing gear
32. Tent
33. Hammock
34. Sleeping bag
35. Sleeping pad
36. Stainless steel pot/frying pan
37. Saw
38. Hatchet
39. Foldable bow saw

Real-life examples and importance of items

Here are real-life examples and the importance of the items listed above:

1. Carabiner clips: In the aftermath of Hurricane Katrina, many people used carabiner clips to secure their belongings or create makeshift shelters using tarps.
2. Emergency blanket: During the 2010 Haiti earthquake, emergency blankets were essential for keeping survivors warm and protected from the elements.
3. Waterproof notepad and pen: In the 2011 Japan tsunami, many survivors used waterproof notepads and pens to leave messages for their loved ones, providing crucial information about their whereabouts and condition.
4. Pack solar charger: In the aftermath of Hurricane Sandy, people relied on solar chargers to keep their phones and other electronic devices charged, helping them stay connected with family and emergency services.
5. Trioxane fuel bars: These fuel bars are essential for starting fires in damp or wet conditions, providing warmth, and cooking food. They were invaluable during the 2013 Colorado floods when many people were left stranded without access to electricity or traditional cooking methods.

Preparing for emergencies and natural disasters is crucial to ensure your safety and well-being. By utilizing the websites listed above, stocking up on essential canned and dried goods, and assembling a well-equipped emergency backpack, you will be better prepared to face any challenges that may come your way. Remember to regularly review and update your supplies and equipment to ensure they remain in good condition and ready for use when needed.

CHAPTER 16

THE JOURNEY TO SELF-RELIANCE OVERCOMING CHALLENGES AND EMBRACING TECHNOLOGY

Embarking on the journey of self-reliance takes time, effort, and financial investment. However, just because you're on a budget doesn't mean you can't start preparing for your family's future. You are in total control, and with some guidance, you can set yourself on the right path to success.

In today's world, technology is a game changer. If you need information on any subject, it's available at your fingertips. For example, preserving food or learning a new skill can be easily found online. To make the most of your budget, do your homework and compare prices before purchasing items. Don't just rely on one website, explore multiple sources to find the best deals.

As you begin your journey, avoid getting overwhelmed by the abundance of information on the Internet. Instead, focus on finding products that meet your needs, suit your budget, and can be upgraded later if necessary. Remember, there are many ways to improvise and adapt items to suit your purposes if you're resourceful and you use common sense.

By learning from the mistakes of others, you can avoid wasting time and money on inadequate solutions. Always be on the lookout for better deals or consider waiting for sales to stretch your budget even further.

The goal of this book is to empower readers to take charge of their lives and provide for their families in any given situation. By developing the skills to handle both mental and physical challenges, you can become more resilient and adaptable, regardless of your financial situation. The first step is the hardest, but with determination and focus, you can accomplish anything.

1. During Hurricane Katrina, many people had to rely on their resourcefulness and improvisational skills to survive and protect their families.
2. In the 2010 Haiti earthquake, survivors who had prepared for emergencies fared better, both physically and emotionally, than those who had not.
3. The 2020 COVID-19 pandemic highlighted the need for self-sufficiency, as supply chains were disrupted, and people had to adapt quickly to changing circumstances.

In conclusion, thank you for taking the time to read this book. It is my hope that it has provided valuable insights and sparked a passion for self-reliance. Regardless of your budget, you can take steps toward a more self-sufficient and secure future for you and your family. Please feel free to check out my YouTube channel at Survival Preparedness for Beginners also for a lot more information and video guides to help you prepare. Thank you, Charles aka Survival Preparedness for Beginners.

Charles is an experienced survivalist and author, who has a YouTube channel called Survival Preparedness for Beginners, with over 7.5 million views and over 1,100 videos over the last four years and who has finally written his first book titled *The Ultimate Survival Guide for Beginners*. The book is an informative guide that covers the basics of emergency preparedness, helping beginners prepare for any type of natural or man-made disaster, prolonged illness, or unforeseeable event.

As a child, Charles experienced the blizzard of 1978, where his family was unprepared for the snowstorm. His father and neighbor had to walk a mile to a store to get food, milk, and bread, and it took them almost six hours to return, dredging through four feet of snow in high winds. Similarly, in 2011, Charles was living in Vermont when Hurricane Irene came through, and he and his family were trapped in their town with no way in or out. His firsthand experience of these situations and others makes him well-equipped to share his knowledge on emergency preparedness.

Charles stresses the importance of being financially and mentally prepared for any circumstance. He highlights catastrophic events of the past, such as Hurricane Katrina in 2005, Hurricane Michael in 2018, and the wildfires in the west, which left millions of people displaced and struggling to find food and shelter. He reminds readers that relying on the government for help during emergencies is not always the best solution, as they may be stretched thin with everything that is going on, both domestically and globally.

In his book, Charles offers practical advice on how to maintain a calm and cool attitude during an emergency, how to store food and water, and what kind of supplies are essential for survival. He provides basic checklists and offers ideas on saving money and where to find good deals on survival gear. Charles's experience in emergency preparedness, camping, hiking, fishing, and hunting for most of his life has helped him to understand how to stay alive in not only the wilderness but also in your own home, and he shares his expertise in the book.

The book addresses various topics, such as how much food and water to store, how to store them, what supplies are needed, and whether to stay put or leave. Charles also provides guidance on where to go in the event of an emergency. He emphasizes that being prepared is a journey that takes time, effort, and resources and encourages readers to take small steps toward preparedness.

Charles's book *The Ultimate Survival Guide for Beginners* is an essential guide for anyone who wants to be prepared for emergencies or disasters. His personal experiences, expertise, and recommendations provide valuable insights and advice for readers. The book serves as an invaluable resource for those looking to ensure their own survival and the survival of their loved ones in times of crisis.